W9-AMO-349

THE BRUMBACK LIBRARY

OF VAN WERT COUNTY

VAN WERT, OHIO

A COLONY LEADER

ROGER
WILLIAMS

BY HELEN STONE PETERSON

ILLUSTRATED BY RAY BURNS

S
J B
W 67 p

GARRARD PUBLISHING COMPANY
CHAMPAIGN, ILLINOIS

For courageous Arthur Jr.

Contents

1. In England

"London Bridge is broken down," hummed nine-year-old Roger Williams as he skipped along the crooked, narrow street in London. He was on his way home from school, this March day in 1612.

As far back as Roger could remember, his mother had sung the song to him. He knew many verses. He sang softly.

> "London Bridge is broken down
> Dance o'er my Lady Lee
> London Bridge is broken down
> With a gay lady."

Suddenly Roger stopped singing. He smelled smoke. He heard shouts. A girl came running from the direction of the fairgrounds. As she rushed past Roger she cried out, "Oh, the King's men are burning poor Preacher Legate to death! Crowds of people are there, watching!"

Horrified, Roger broke into a run. In a few minutes he reached his home where he lived with his parents, his older brother and sister, and his younger brother. His father, a tailor, had a shop in the front room.

Roger found his mother alone, waiting for him. She threw her arms around the weeping boy. "Hush, hush."

"Do you know what's happening?" he asked.

His mother nodded.

Just then Roger's father entered the room. "Mr. Legate was a heretic, preaching against our religion and against our Church of England," he said.

"God isn't pleased to have him killed for his religion. The Bible says to love," sobbed Roger.

His father's voice was very stern. "Mr. Legate would be alive if he had taken back the wicked and dangerous things he preached. Since he refused, he was considered a traitor. Our church is part of our government, and King James is the head of both. That's the way it is."

After a while Roger wiped away his tears.

His father spoke more gently. "Come with me. I must deliver some cloth."

They took Roger's favorite walk along the Thames River. The river was full of rowboats and ferries carrying people up and down and from shore to shore. Farther down the river, past London Bridge, large ships were anchored. Roger stopped to watch a ship whose sailors were getting ready to leave port.

One sailor called out merrily to Roger, "We're off to America! Shall I bring you back a codfish? Or a bundle of furs from the Indians?"

Roger smiled gravely. He knew that trading ships and fishing ships sailed along the Atlantic coast of America. And he knew many brave Englishmen had died trying to start colonies in the wilderness there. But now England had a successful colony which was five years old. It was Jamestown in Virginia.

The ship, its white sails spread, began to move away in the breeze. The sailor waved good-bye. "Remember," he shouted, "the New World is the promised land!"

All of a sudden Roger felt better. Smiling almost gaily, he waved to the sailor. And he said to himself, "Yes! There is a New World. There will be new ways too."

2. "My Son"

One Sunday, when Roger was fourteen, he sat with his family in St. Sepulchre's Church. He was copying down the sermon in shorthand. Roger often did that. At home he compared what the minister said with what was written in the Bible.

Roger loved to study his Bible. He believed every word in it was the Word of God.

This Sunday, after the service, a gentleman motioned for Roger to come to his pew. "Sir Edward Coke!" the boy told himself, and his face lighted up. Coke, now in his sixties, was one of the greatest lawyers in England.

Sir Edward looked through Roger's shorthand notebook. "Come to court tomorrow, will you please? I wish to talk with you about working for me."

"Oh yes, sir," said Roger, his eyes sparkling.

Roger had finished grammar school where a kind of shorthand was one of his subjects. His father had made no further plans for his education. A boy had little hope of more schooling when his father was a tailor.

"What will I do?" That question had been running through Roger's mind for some time. His older brother was learning the tailor's trade. His sister was going to marry a tailor.

"I'll not be a tailor," Roger had decided. But he hadn't made up his mind what he would be.

Roger kept his appointment with Sir Edward. "How would you like to make a record for me of some cases I'm handling in court?" the famous lawyer asked. "You could take the speeches in shorthand and write copies afterwards."

A happy smile swept over Roger's face. "I will do my best," he replied.

Roger went to work, writing out the speeches both carefully and quickly. Sir Edward was highly pleased. He grew very fond of the bright boy.

"My son," the great man often called Roger.

Soon Roger knew what he wanted to do. "I want to go to college some day and get a good education the way Sir Edward did," he said to himself. But would he ever have enough money?

Besides, he hadn't studied the subjects required for college entrance.

Roger continued to work for Coke during the next few years. The boy saw the lawyer dare to stand up to powerful King James I. The King believed the people had only the rights he chose to give to them. But Coke kept protesting, "The law gives some rights to the people! Even kings must obey the law!"

When the famous lawyer became a member of Parliament, he took the lead in declaring Parliament's rights. Parliament was the branch of the government which helped make the laws. "Every member has the right of freedom of speech," wrote Coke with great courage.

King James was furious. He didn't want any members of Parliament asking him questions or criticizing his rule. He punished Coke by sending him to prison for nine months.

Just before Sir Edward went off to prison, he opened the door to a new life for Roger. "I have secured a scholarship for you at Charterhouse School. You can prepare for college there. If you do well, the school will give you a scholarship for college."

A lump came into Roger's throat. He couldn't put into words all that he felt. He thanked Sir

Edward. "I will study very hard," he promised. Charterhouse was close to Roger's home. His chief subjects were Latin, Greek, and religion. He was one of the best students there, and earned a scholarship to the University of Cambridge.

While he was studying at the university, Roger made up his mind about his future. "I will be a Puritan minister," he decided.

Roger had been a Puritan since he was a boy. Puritans belonged to the Church of England, but they tried to follow the exact words of the Bible. So they wanted to remove some of the ceremonies from the church, because these were not mentioned in the Bible. "They're trying to make the church pure," other people said. "They're Puritans."

Coke wasn't a Puritan. When he learned of Roger's plan, he had a talk with him. "You know the King rules both the church and the government. And you know he despises Puritans. If you preach anything he doesn't like, you will be silenced or perhaps even punished. What will your future be?"

"God will direct my steps," Roger replied.

He saw very little of elderly Sir Edward after that, but he never forgot the great man. Many years later Roger wrote, "His example . . . spurred me on."

3. Puritan Minister

"Mr. Williams, welcome to Otes," said Lady Masham. She led the way to one of the parlors in her beautiful home.

Roger had completed his work at the university. He had been hired as the chaplain, or minister, at Otes. This was the large country estate of Sir William Masham. He was a member of Parliament and also a Puritan.

Two pretty young ladies entered the parlor. Lady Masham introduced them. "My daughter Joan and her companion Mary Barnard." Mary worked for the family. Young ladies from good homes, like Mary, could learn a great deal working in the house of a nobleman.

Roger started his duties at once. He began each day by leading the family in prayer. At the end of the day he read the Bible to them. On Sundays he preached a sermon in their lovely chapel. House guests joined these family gatherings. Everyone liked the charming minister.

Men serving in Parliament with Sir William were frequent guests at Otes. Among them was Oliver Cromwell, a cousin of Lady Masham. Until recently young Cromwell had been an unsuccessful farmer. No one dreamed that one day he would be the most powerful man in England.

Roger listened as these leaders talked about Charles I who was now King. "He's worse than his father James was! He won't call Parliament into session because he wants all the power in his own hands. And he hates the Puritans. He has spies everywhere, fining Puritan ministers and throwing them into jail."

Some of Sir William's friends were organizing the Massachusetts Bay Company to settle Puritans in New England. Though King Charles did not like the Puritans, he wanted colonies. So he gave the company a charter granting permission for the formation of the Massachusetts Bay Colony. Roger met Mr. John Winthrop, a wealthy lawyer who would be the colony's first governor.

There were already two settlements in New England. A small group of Puritans had recently started Salem. Plymouth Colony, where the Pilgrims lived, was nine years old.

One day Sir William came hurrying home from London. "Oh, Mr. Williams!" he cried. "I saw a terrible sight in London—a man with his nose slit and both his ears cut off. The King's men punished him in this dreadful way because of the things he said against the Church of England."

"Such torture is wicked!" protested Roger hotly. "The King will do anything to keep his Church of England strong. He is stamping out every religious difference."

Sir William was devoted to Roger. There was deep concern now in Sir William's voice. "All Puritan ministers are in danger. Governor Winthrop will be taking settlers to New England early next year. Have you considered going?"

"I have been thinking about it," replied Roger. He also had been thinking about separating completely from the Church of England. He was beginning to feel that he couldn't remain within the national church controlled by the King.

Roger became ill a few months later. Mary Barnard helped nurse him, carrying hot broth and medicine to him. Her smile was like sunshine.

"How cheerful you are," Roger remarked one day.

Mary answered him by quoting a verse from the Bible. "A merry heart doeth good like a medicine."

"That's true." Roger laughed and felt better.

He fell in love with Mary. When he was well again, he asked her to marry him. Their wedding took place in December, 1629, at the nearby church. Roger was then 26 years old, and Mary was 20.

In the spring, Governor Winthrop sailed for Massachusetts. His fleet of ships carried hundreds of people as well as horses, cows, and supplies. Other ships would follow. Many Puritan families were eager to cross the ocean for they wanted freedom to worship in their own way.

"We will go," Roger and Mary decided. They made plans to sail with a later group of settlers. Roger also decided to separate from the Church of England.

They felt a pang when the time came to say good-bye to all their dear friends at Otes. They then traveled to London to say a sad good-bye to Roger's mother. His father had died and the rest of the family was scattered. Roger never saw his mother again for she died a few years later.

Roger and Mary sailed from England on the ship *Lyon* in December, 1630. There were only 20 passengers on it, but the ship was loaded with wheat, peas, oatmeal, and other supplies for the Massachusetts Bay Colony.

As the ship left the Old World behind, Roger thought about the future. "The New World holds so much promise," he told himself. He felt a surge of joy. "Best of all, it holds the promise of freedom."

4. In New England

About two months later, after a stormy voyage, Roger and Mary caught sight of the rounded hills and forests of New England. Mary gazed at the wilderness stretching before them. Then she asked, "Where will our home be?"

"I don't know," Roger answered gently.

They landed at the tiny settlement of Boston. It was one of several settlements scattered around Massachusetts Bay.

The people of Boston were living along the harbor shore. Some had huts. Others had only sailcloth tents to shelter them from the snow and howling wind. Mary tried hard not to shudder as she looked about.

Roger comforted her. "Better houses will soon be built," he said.

Governor Winthrop welcomed them with joy. "The supplies aboard the *Lyon* will save our colony!" he said. "Many people are sick, and some are half-starved. Now they will soon feel better."

He told Roger and Mary to move in with a family who had a large hut. It was crowded, but at least it was warmer than a tent.

One day, not long afterwards, Roger saw a man being whipped. "He is being punished for Sabbath-breaking," one of the Governor's assistants explained. "Instead of going to church, this rascal went after a wild turkey for his dinner."

Roger felt sick at heart. "Where is the new way?" he asked himself. "Here the church is part of the government just as it is in England."

Roger knew that all the settlers weren't Puritans. Some had come in the hope of making a better living, rather than for any religious reason. But the Puritan governor and his assistants, together with the Puritan ministers, held the power.

Soon Governor Winthrop asked Roger to be minister of the Boston church. It took courage for Roger to give his answer to the dignified older man. "I cannot be your minister because your church has not separated from the Church of England."

Governor Winthrop was startled. "Of course not! If we should separate, King Charles would take away our charter and our colony would fail. Have you separated from the Church of England?"

"Yes," replied Roger.

Roger dared to say more. "I believe it's wrong for your government to force people to follow your religion."

Governor Winthrop looked shocked. He spoke coldly. "We know God's will and our laws shall uphold it. People can leave this colony if they don't want to be one of us."

So Roger and Mary moved to Salem, a town north of Boston. Roger became assistant minister in the Salem church, some of whose members favored separation from the Church of England. He stayed only a few months. Salem was part of the Massachusetts Bay Colony and the colony leaders frowned on Roger's appointment.

Before summer's end Roger and Mary were settled with the Pilgrims in Plymouth, about 38 miles south of Boston. Plymouth was independent of the Bay Colony, and its church had separated from the Church of England. Roger was appointed the assistant minister. On Sundays he and Mary marched with the Pilgrims to the fort which also served as their church.

Roger was given a small house in the little town. And he was given land where he raised food for Mary and himself. "I wrought hard at the hoe," he wrote.

The Wampanoag Indians lived nearby. Friendly Massasoit was their chief. Roger spent all of his spare time with them, working hard to learn their language. Most Englishmen did not bother to learn the difficult Indian words.

The Indians took Roger out to sea in their canoes. While they fished together, Roger listened

to the Indians' bitter complaints. "The English-men have pushed us out of the bay which has the best lobsters. They let their pigs dig up our clams. And they're taking more and more of our hunting grounds for their crops and pastures."

The Narragansett Indians lived to the west, on the other side of Narragansett Bay. By the second year Roger was visiting them too. He became good friends with the two chiefs—old Canonicus and his young nephew Miantonomo. Tall, proud Miantonomo reminded Roger of a prince.

Sometimes Canonicus spoke about his fear for the future of the Indians. "Why are more and more shiploads of Englishmen coming to these shores? And why do they bring so many terrible guns?"

Roger thought about these problems. "The Indians have rights to this land," he told Mary. "It does not belong to the King of England to give away. First of all the land should have been bought from the Indians."

Roger put his ideas in writing for the leaders of Plymouth to read. They disagreed with Roger, and things didn't go smoothly for him after that. He knew he must leave.

"Our home won't be in Plymouth," Roger said gently to Mary.

5. Banishment!

Roger and Mary moved back to Salem. They had friends there. And they had a baby daughter now, named for Mary.

When Roger again became the assistant minister of the Salem church, the colony leaders in Boston were much alarmed. "We must watch him closely," they decided. "He has opinions which are dangerous to the success of our colony, and he will spread them through his preaching."

The next year the Salem minister died and Roger was given the position. Leaders in Boston grew even more alarmed. A few months later Roger was ordered into the General Court.

"You are preaching that our churches should separate from the Church of England. You are preaching that it's wrong for the government to punish people for Sabbath breaking." And the list went on. Roger was warned, "Stop! Or you will be punished!"

Roger knew how harshly the leaders punished people who were found guilty. One man had had his ears cut off after he had talked against the church and the government. Others had been shipped back to England.

Roger had courage and continued preaching freely. He was a lively speaker and won followers.

In October, 1635, Roger was brought to trial.

The trial was held in a church with a dirt floor at Newtown, later called Cambridge, Massachusetts. The officers of the colony were there, and twelve ministers. Roger had a sudden memory of Sir Edward Coke standing up to powerful King James I.

Alone and unafraid, Roger defended himself. But he was found guilty of spreading new and dangerous opinions. His sentence was banishment. He must leave the colony by spring.

Back home, Roger comforted Mary. "God will direct our steps," he said gently.

Later that same month their second daughter was born. "Some day in this land of ours, a person will be free to worship as he chooses," Roger said to Mary. "I would like to name our daughter Freeborn." And they did.

Suddenly, one very cold day in January, Roger learned that men were coming to seize him. Roger's followers had been visiting his home, so the colony leaders concluded that he was still spreading his dangerous opinions. They all decided to ship him to England on a boat which was ready to sail.

Quickly Roger decided to escape. "I'll flee to Massasoit and my Wampanoag Indian friends, Mary. They'll take me in."

She gasped. Roger was weak from a recent illness. He would have to walk for four days or more through the snow-covered wilderness.

Tears sprang to Mary's eyes. "Where will you sleep?"

"I'll find a hollow tree. Don't be afraid for me."

Mary felt a blast of icy wind hit the house. She saw that snow was falling thickly. "You will freeze to death," she sobbed.

"I am in the hands of our Father in Heaven," Roger answered gently.

He kissed his little girls good-bye. He hugged Mary, whispering, "I'll make a home and send for you just as soon as I can." Taking a small packet of food, he slipped away into the woods.

When Roger finally stumbled into Massasoit's wigwam, he looked more dead than alive. "Welcome," said the chief, leading him to the fire.

Roger lived with his Wampanoag friends and grew well and strong. In the early spring three men, who had been among his followers in Salem, and two youths came to Roger. They brought tools and seeds, and goods to trade with the Indians.

"We want to make our homes wherever you settle," the men said. Roger agreed to this.

They started to build houses on land Roger bought from Massasoit. They planted some seeds. Then one day a runner appeared with this message from Plymouth Colony:

"You must move, for that land was granted to us by England. Perhaps you can live in the Narragansett territory. Their land doesn't belong to us or to the Bay Colony."

"I'm banished again," thought Roger. So he asked the men to pack and be ready to move when he returned. He hurried to his friends Canonicus and Miantonomo, the two Narragansett chiefs. Just recently he had traveled back and forth between them and the Wampanoags, settling a quarrel.

Now the chiefs listened to Roger and nodded their approval. "We will be pleased to have you for our neighbor," said old Canonicus. But he didn't want to be paid in money or goods.

"We want peaceful neighbors around us. You will pay us by working to keep peace," said Canonicus.

Princely Miantonomo smiled. "Yes, you will be our peacemaker."

6. Providence

Roger went back for his companions. They paddled their canoe down the Seekonk River to the northern tip of Narragansett Bay. Then they paddled up the arm of the Bay called the Great Salt River. They landed near a spring of fine drinking water. This was the place Roger chose for his settlement.

He bowed his head. "I name this place Providence in a sense of God's merciful providence unto me," he said. It was April, 1636.

Miantonomo, with some of his Indians, was there to welcome Roger and his companions. Over a campfire the Indians cooked fish and succotash made from corn and beans. They all feasted happily together.

Afterwards Miantonomo gave Roger a basket of seed corn. "Come," he said. "I will show you where to plant."

The two men climbed the hill in back of the spring. Miantonomo pointed to cleared fields the Indians were not using that season. "There," he said.

From the hilltop Roger had a good view of the countryside. He looked down at the Great Salt River with its beds of clams and oysters. He noticed huckleberry bushes growing around the fields, and remembered the delicious huckleberry pudding the Indian women had often given him to eat. He gazed at the thick forests stretching on and on, filled with deer and beaver and giant trees.

A feeling of freedom and joy swept over Roger. "Oh, Miantonomo, thank you for everything."

Roger and his companions planted the corn and put up a bark shed for a temporary sleeping place. Then they started building their homes along the shore. They placed them side-by-side so the families could help each other when necessary. Their farming land was a distance away.

Soon several more settlers came from Salem, herding a few pigs and goats along the Indian trails. The animals were turned loose on islands in the bay. They would find enough to eat there and wolves couldn't catch them.

The settlers worked hard but they were short of almost everything. No ship brought supplies the way the *Lyon* and so many other ships did to Boston. No rich company, like the Massachusetts Bay Company, helped Providence. It would be some time before the settlers could afford expensive animals like cows, horses, and sheep.

"I know what it is to tug at the oar, to dig with the spade, and to labor . . . day and night," Roger wrote.

That summer, even before all the houses were finished, Roger took steps to start a government. He called town meetings of the men who were heads of families. By a majority vote the men decided on the rules for group living. Providence now had a government of the people and by the people.

Roger gave away all of his land to the town. "It was mine as truly as any man's coat upon his back," he wrote later. Arrangements were made so that future settlers could buy land from the town.

At the end of the summer, Roger's family

arrived along with some other families. There were now 32 people in Providence. Roger flung his arms around his wife, three-year-old Mary, and the baby.

"You're home," he said.

Eagerly Roger took his family through their house. It had a large room downstairs. At one end there was a huge fireplace where Mary would do the cooking. Smiling, Mary touched the table and benches and wooden plates Roger had made. She saw the ladder which led to the sleeping room upstairs.

Mary's eyes were shining. "Everything is lovely," she said. "Providence is a good place to be."

The next Sunday a church service was held in their home. Roger preached the sermon. "We'll hold a service here each Sunday," Roger and Mary agreed. All the settlers were invited, but no one was forced to come.

Nobody in Providence was ever whipped, banished, or had his ears cut off for religious reasons. Roger separated the church from the government; one was never a part of the other. Later this became known as the separation of church and state.

Providence had religious freedom. Roger was the leader of a new way.

7. Peacemaker

One day soon after Mary arrived, Roger received a frantic message from the Massachusetts Bay Colony. "The Pequot chiefs are urging the Narragansett Indians to unite with them for the purpose of fighting us. You must try to prevent this!"

"I'm going to the Narragansetts right now," Roger told Mary.

He grabbed his jacket and the other things he would need. As Mary watched him hurry away, tears flooded her eyes. "Such a good, forgiving man," she murmured to herself. "That message for help came from the colony which banished him."

It was the fall of 1636. The powerful Pequots lived in Connecticut where an English colony was just getting started. None of the colonies in New England were strong yet. If the Indians united and fought now, it was likely they could wipe out the English.

Roger traveled swiftly by canoe and on foot. He found the chiefs of both tribes in the council house of the Narragansetts, sitting on floor mats. After a welcoming nod from Canonicus, Roger joined the circle.

He listened to the speeches of the Pequot chiefs. "You see how grasping the English are. Right before our eyes they are taking more and more of our land. We must stop them now, or they won't leave us space to spread our blankets."

Canonicus asked Roger to speak.

"The English can bring more guns and more soldiers from across the ocean," said Roger. "Then there would be a terrible war. Let us all live together as loving neighbors, instead."

"Your talk is like a woman's!" thundered the Pequots.

That night some fierce Pequot chiefs entered the wigwam where Roger had lain down to sleep. Their faces were dark with anger.

"What are they going to do?" Roger wondered.

He heard one chief mutter, "We will boil him in a kettle."

Roger saw that each chief carried a sharp knife. As the chiefs stretched out beside Roger, his heart pounded. "They will try to kill me," he thought.

But the Narragansetts were watching over their friend and no harm came to him.

Two days later Canonicus and Miantonomo announced their decision that the Narragansetts would not fight the Englishmen. And Canonicus warned the Pequot chiefs, "Hush your talk of war. War is always sad and mournful. It is so for the loser and often so for the winner."

That winter the Pequots killed some settlers who lived in lonely places. By spring the English decided to put an end to such murders. They made a surprise attack on the large fort where the Pequots were living, and set fire to it. Indian men, women, and children were burned to death. A few remaining Pequots were made slaves in Massachusetts or sold as slaves in Bermuda. As a tribe the Pequots were wiped out.

"The horror was carried too far," Roger mourned. He wrote to the Bay Colony. "God delights in mercy!"

The Narragansetts were now the most powerful

tribe in New England. When there was trouble from any of the Indians, the English were quick to blame the Narragansetts. "That's because the English are afraid of them," Roger thought.

Mary grew accustomed to seeing Roger hurry away to his Narragansett friends. He was determined to help them keep peace. He walked with the Narragansetts to Connecticut to make a treaty with the colonists and the Indians there. He wrote many letters for the Narragansetts to the leaders of the Massachusetts Bay Colony and of Plymouth. He talked with agents from those two colonies. Year after year Roger continued his work as peacemaker.

"I spared neither purse nor pains that the whole land, English and natives, might sleep in peace," Roger wrote.

8. Danger

"Religious freedom is the precious jewel of our settlement," Roger said again and again to Mary.

The year after the Pequot War, Roger welcomed a group of people who had been banished by the Massachusetts Bay Colony. Their religion, called Antinomianism, was a little different from the Puritan religion permitted in Boston. Mr. William Coddington, a rich merchant, was one of their leaders. The newcomers wanted to live on the big island in Narragansett Bay.

"We call it Rhode Island," Roger told them. "It's named after the island of Rhodes in Greece. And like Rhodes, our beautiful island is covered with roses."

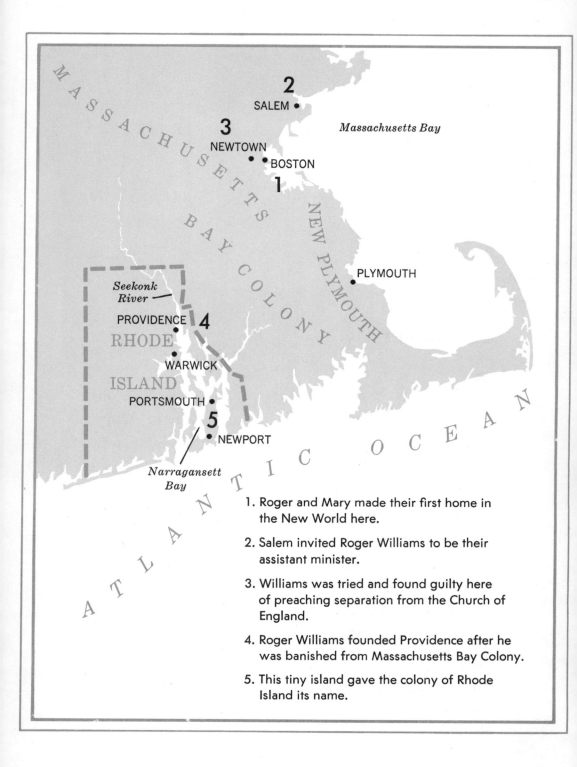

MASSACHUSETTS BAY COLONY

NEW PLYMOUTH

ATLANTIC OCEAN

Massachusetts Bay

2
SALEM •

3
NEWTOWN •
• BOSTON
1

• PLYMOUTH

Seekonk River

PROVIDENCE • **4**

RHODE

WARWICK •

ISLAND

PORTSMOUTH •

5
• NEWPORT

Narragansett Bay

1. Roger and Mary made their first home in the New World here.

2. Salem invited Roger Williams to be their assistant minister.

3. Williams was tried and found guilty here of preaching separation from the Church of England.

4. Roger Williams founded Providence after he was banished from Massachusetts Bay Colony.

5. This tiny island gave the colony of Rhode Island its name.

The island belonged to the Narragansett Indians. Roger talked with Canonicus and Miantonomo. The chiefs agreed to sell the island to the newcomers, but only because Roger was their friend. Strangers couldn't have bought it at any price.

"Rhode Island was obtained by love," Roger wrote later.

The newcomers moved onto the island, first settling Portsmouth and later, Newport. Some people in Providence took a dislike to Mr. Coddington. "He doesn't want to be just a farmer," they pointed out. "He wants to live like a king, and the time will come when he'll make trouble."

Roger welcomed the Baptists too. They fled from the Bay Colony where they weren't permitted to worship as they pleased. In Providence, in 1639, they organized the first Baptist Church in America. Roger worshiped with them.

But soon Roger made up his mind that he couldn't be limited by the belief of any one church group. He took the name Seeker for his religion. He put it this way—"I am forever seeking God's truth."

By 1640 there were 120 settlers in Providence, clearing land and farming, and trading with captains of the small sailing ships which now came into Narragansett Bay. The settlers had all the religious freedom they desired. But a few people were hard to get along with and they were quarrelsome. Others schemed to get the best land. So there were some angry arguments.

In 1642 trouble broke out among settlers who had gone to live on the farming land south of Providence. "We don't want to be part of Providence any longer," a few disloyal men shouted. "We want this land to be part of Massachusetts." So they wrote to the Massachusetts Bay Colony, making that request.

The leaders in Massachusetts agreed to govern the area. It had grown more valuable since the fierce Pequots had been wiped out. Massachusetts wanted the land and a harbor on Narragansett Bay for their trading ships.

There was an uproar in the rest of Providence and on the big island. "The Massachusetts Bay Colony will swallow us up just the way big fish swallow the small fish," the people cried. "What can we do to protect ourselves?"

Town meetings were held. "We must get a charter for our colony from the government in England," the people decided. "A charter will establish our rights to this land." But could they get one? The people asked Roger to try.

"I've got to go to England," Roger told Mary. "I'd give my life to save our religious freedom."

Mary understood. How she and the children would miss Roger, though! By this time there were two sons, Providence and Daniel, and another daughter, Mercy.

Before he left, Roger hurried to his Indian friends. Old Canonicus looked sad as he said farewell, for Roger was the only Englishman he trusted.

He reminded Roger, "I have never suffered any wrong to be done to the English since they landed."

"I know," said Roger.

"Will they treat us well?" Canonicus asked. "Will they let us live in peace while you are gone?"

"That will be my prayer to the blessed God of peace," Roger replied.

Young Chief Miantonomo smiled warmly at Roger. "We need you here to help us deal with our English neighbors. Come back to us soon. Good-bye, my friend."

9. In England Again

Roger was not allowed to board any ship in Boston harbor because he had been banished from the Massachusetts Bay Colony. So he sailed from Dutch New Amsterdam in the spring of 1643.

While he was crossing the ocean, Roger wrote a book. He hoped that other Englishmen would learn the language of the Indians. He put down Indian words, phrases, and sentences, and gave their meanings. When he finished, Roger had a book which covered much more than language. It was the story of how the Indians in New England lived.

"They hold the band of brotherhood dear," Roger wrote. "There are no beggars amongst them, nor fatherless children unprovided for."

Roger told how much the Indian boys enjoyed their foot races. They were excellent runners by the time they were young men. "I have known many of them to run between fourscore and a hundred miles in a summer's day," Roger wrote.

He described the delight the Indians took in their games. "They have great meetings of football playing . . . town against town, upon some broad sandy shore."

Roger put this little poem in his book too:

"Oft have I heard these Indians say
These English will deceive us.
Of all that's ours, our lands and lives
In the end they will bereave us."

A Key into the Language of America was the title Roger chose for his book. "I'll give it to a printer as soon as I reach London," he decided. And that's what he did.

How many changes Roger found in England! The nation was having a civil war then. King Charles had tried to rule England completely alone, robbing Parliament and the people of their rights. Now many Englishmen were fighting to get back their rights, and members of Parliament were leading the fight against the King.

Parliament held London and carried on its meetings there. Roger learned that the King was with his army northwest of the city.

Roger also learned that the Massachusetts Bay Colony had agents in London working to get a charter for all the Narragansett land. "I'm in a race for the charter," thought Roger. "Massachusetts reminds me of a greedy person who has platters full of dainties, yet snatches crusts from the poor."

Roger went to the Parliament building and looked up Sir William Masham. Sir William was delighted to see his former chaplain. Roger knew some members of Parliament and Sir William introduced him to other members. Roger talked earnestly with all these influential men about the charter he wanted.

As the war continued on through the winter months, Parliament gained in power over the King. The members decided they had the right to award the charter. Roger's book now had been published. Full of curiosity about the Indians, people read it eagerly.

"There has been no book like this from Massachusetts," said members of Parliament. The book convinced some of them that Roger should get the charter.

The race with Massachusetts was close, but Roger won by two votes. He got the charter for the Providence Plantations in Narragansett Bay.

Just before leaving England, Roger had another book printed, *The Bloudy Tenent of Persecution*. In it Roger pleaded for religious freedom, and for separation of church and state. He upheld the rights of the people. "The foundation of all civil power lies in the people," he wrote.

In later years Roger wrote more books and pamphlets. But *The Bloudy Tenent of Persecution* became known as his masterpiece.

10. The Charter

Roger landed at Boston in September, 1644. The officers did not bother him after he showed a safe-conduct pass from Parliament.

Roger felt a rush of joy as he started walking down the long trail toward Providence. He could hardly wait to see Mary and his children. A new baby, Joseph, had been born while he was away.

When Roger finally tramped out of the woods at the Seekonk River, wild cheers filled the air. "Hip, hip, hooray! Hooray for Roger Williams, Roger Williams!"

There in fourteen canoes were Roger's neighbors. A runner had brought the news that Roger was returning, and men from Providence had come to welcome him.

Surprised, Roger stared at his friends. More shouts of greeting went up. Roger's eyes lighted with pleasure, and he burst into merry laughter.

Cheering and laughing, the men paddled Roger home.

After a happy reunion with his family, Roger hurried off to Canonicus. It was one of the saddest journeys of his life. Miantonomo had been murdered while Roger was in England.

In a battle with another tribe, Miantonomo had been captured. His captor had then sent a message to Boston, where the leaders of New England were meeting. He asked them what to do with the young chief. The leaders replied that Miantonomo ought to be put to death.

Roger found Canonicus looking very old and weary, and weighed down with sorrow. "I too grieve," said Roger, choking back a sob. "Miantonomo was my kind friend."

The two men had a long talk. Before it ended, Canonicus made a request. "It would please me if you would live nearer to us. You could build a trading house close by. Will you?"

"Yes," replied Roger.

He had done some trading with the Indians ever since his years in Plymouth, but he needed to do more now. He had a large family to care

for. And he had to pay back money he had borrowed for his trip to England. So he built his trading house on the shore of Narragansett Bay, some miles below Providence. It was a beautiful spot.

The Indians brought furs to the trading house. Roger paid them in supplies they needed, such as hoes, kettles, and cloth. He sold the furs to trading boats which came by.

Roger could not spend as much time at the trading house as he wished. Now that the colony had a charter, the towns must unite under one central government. Roger called the people together in town meetings. There the people talked about what rights the towns themselves would keep, and what powers would be given to the central government.

Mr. Coddington at Newport made Roger's job more difficult. He had a beautiful estate stocked with the finest horses and cows and sheep. The farmers on the mainland, working from dawn to dark, had nothing to compare with it. They had plenty of pigs and goats, but other farm animals were still scarce.

"I don't want any connection with the mainland. Too many people there are riffraff," Mr. Coddington told Newport residents. But the majority of them decided that Newport would join together with the other towns.

Almost three years passed while the townspeople talked things over. Then in May, 1647, delegates from Providence, Warwick, Portsmouth and Newport met at Portsmouth. Warwick was a new town on the mainland. Roger was the leader of the group from Providence.

The delegates organized the central government of the colony. "The form of government . . . is Democratical," they wrote in their official record.

Religious freedom was guaranteed. "All men may walk as their consciences persuade them, every man in the name of his God."

Roger's way had become the way of the whole colony.

11. Treason

After the union of the towns, men other than Roger accepted important offices in the colony. So Roger had more time for his trading house. That summer he took his family there.

As soon as they arrived, some Indian girls and boys appeared. They invited the older Williams children to pick strawberries with them. "We know an open place in the woods where there are enough ripe strawberries to fill a ship," they said. Laughing, the youngsters ran off together.

When they returned, their baskets were filled with red, juicy, sweet strawberries. Mary mashed some of the fruit and she pounded corn into meal. Then she made loaves of strawberry bread the way the Indian women had taught her.

"It tastes grand," her children told her.

And they told Roger, "We just love it here."

The trading house became a second home for Roger. He lived right there much of the time, carrying on trade with his Indian friends. His family continued to visit there.

One day Canonicus sent for Roger. The chief was dying of old age. Roger stayed with his friend until the end. Afterwards Roger continued to work as peacemaker, keeping the promise he had made to Canonicus when he first came to Providence.

"Scarcely a week has passed but some way or other I have been used as instrumental to the peace . . . in this country," Roger wrote four years later. It was 1651.

That year the colony was again in terrible trouble. Massachusetts, Plymouth, and Connecticut were not respecting its boundaries. They all were claiming land there.

"Those three colonies are like three wolves after one sheep," Roger told himself.

Then Mr. Coddington returned from a trip to England where he had succeeded in convincing Parliament to appoint him Governor-for-life of the big island. He had separated the island's government from that of the mainland and had split the colony.

"That's treason!" cried many people in all the towns.

They asked Roger to return to England and save their colony. They asked Dr. John Clarke of Newport to go with him. Dr. Clarke, a physician and a Baptist minister, was a fighter for religious freedom.

Roger sold his trading house for very little. His heart was sad when he had to say good-bye to his family again. He sailed away in the fall of 1651.

When he and Dr. Clarke reached England, the civil war was over. King Charles I had been beheaded and Parliament now governed the nation. Roger's powerful friends there helped him all they could.

Nearly a year passed before they finally had good news for Roger. "We have removed Mr. Coddington as Governor-for-life of the island. We have joined your colony together again."

Roger was pleased. "Half our job is done," he told Dr. Clarke. "Now we must get the boundaries confirmed so other colonies can't steal our land."

Parliament was busy, however, and couldn't act on the boundaries. So another year passed. Then Oliver Cromwell became the head of the

English government. He and Roger had known each other from the time Roger was chaplain at Otes.

"We will pass an order that your neighbors are to respect your boundaries," Cromwell promised Roger. His promise was carried out.

In the spring of 1654 Roger sailed for home. Dr. Clarke stayed in England, as agent for the Colony. He would protect its interests during the changing times.

Roger found the colony in chaos. The towns were quarreling with each other and weren't supporting the central government. Roger threw himself into the task of getting the colonists to work together.

12. Mr. President

An election was held and Roger, then 51 years old, was chosen President of the colony.

He was a strong President, determined to bring peace and order. He was in office almost three years. Under his leadership the towns worked together and the colony moved ahead.

Soon after Roger became President, there was trouble between the Narragansett Indians and another tribe. As a result, soldiers from the New England colonies prepared to fight the Narragansetts. How many times Roger had talked both sides out of war!

"There is the possibility of keeping sweet peace in most cases," he had written. "And if it be possible, it is the command of God that peace be kept."

Once more Roger wrote a long letter to the leaders of the Massachusetts Bay Colony about the Narragansetts. "Are not our families grown up in peace amongst them?" he asked. "I cannot learn that ever . . . they stained their hands with any English blood."

One more time the peace was kept.

While Roger was President, the Quakers came to New England. "We forbid you to live here," said the leaders in Massachusetts. They believed that the Quakers' religion was both wrong and dangerous. When the Quakers insisted on staying, they were cruelly punished. Four were hung.

"You're welcome in our colony," said Roger. He didn't agree with the Quakers' religion, but he did believe with all his heart in religious freedom.

Roger also welcomed Jews to the colony. They came from Dutch New Amsterdam where they were not wanted. At Newport, they built the first Jewish synagogue in America.

Six years after Roger left the office of President, faithful Dr. Clarke got a new charter from King Charles II. Charles had become ruler of England, following the death of Oliver Cromwell. The King named the colony "Rhode Island and Providence Plantations." Later, people dropped

the last three words and called the whole colony Rhode Island.

The royal charter confirmed the one Roger had from Parliament. Religious freedom was now guaranteed.

Roger's heart brimmed with joy. "We have more freedom than any other people in the world," he told himself. "We have planted a seed."

Roger lived to be an old man. He needed money in his last years, but he was helped by his sons who were farmers and traders.

"Can you find such another?" Daniel wrote about his father. "He gave away his lands and other estates to them that he thought were most in want, until he gave away all."

No record was kept of Mary's death, and no one wrote down the exact date Roger died. A neighbor sent a letter to a friend in March, 1683, saying, "Mr. Williams is lately deceased." Roger then would have been 80 years old.

Almost 100 years later the United States became a nation. It formed a government of the people and by the people. It had religious freedom, and separation of church and state.

At last, Roger Williams' way had become the American way.